GREAT CARDS

AND TAGS Ideas, Tips & Techniques

GREAT CARDS

AND TAGS Ideas, Tips & Techniques

Leslie Carola

Arena Books Associates, LLC

Copyright © 2008 by Arena Books Associates, LLC
This edition of *Great Cards and Tags: Ideas, Tips & Techniques* has been pre-
pared for Crafter's Choice Book Club by Arena Books Associates, LLC.

ISBN 13: 978-0-9797922-1-2

Book concept and development: Leslie Carola, Arena Books Associates, LLC
Design: Elizabeth Johnsboen
Photographer: Jon Van Gorder

Acknowledgments: Thank you to the contributors—individual designers,
artists, crafters, and manufacturers— who have contributed projects.
Dave Brethauer (www.memoryboxco.com); Andrea Grossman and
Mrs. Grossman's Paper Company (www.mrsgrossmans.com);
Nathalie Métivier, Magenta (www.magentastyle.com);
Judy Ritchie (www.greatamericanstampstore.com); Irene Seifer;
Susan Swan (www.susanswan.com); Christine Timmons; Janet Williams.

Contents

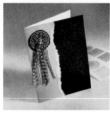

Introduction

Paper is irresistible. We can't seem to do enough to it or with it. We color, bend, fold, roll, tear, stitch, weave, pleat, punch, pierce, wrap, and cut it. We make cards, postcards, and gift tags, ornaments, and even jewelry from paper. We wrap gifts with paper. We scrapbook with paper. And we add decorative accents of all kinds to "lift the projects," to add our own style and visual interest. Who of us hasn't reached out to stroke an elegant sheet of paper, smooth a ruffled piece, or touch a textured one?

If you walk into a retail craft or gift store, or search online, are you overwhelmed by the variety of materials available? It *is* amazing and exciting, but sometimes dizzying to be presented with so many choices. There are *so* many papers, *so* many rubber stamps, punches, color pencils, markers, paints, finishing glazes, texturizers, and seemingly endless embellishments. We are certainly lucky to be paper crafters now with so much right at our fingertips but sometimes the idea you had in the first place can be swept

Susan Swan

away with a cluttering number of other possibilities.

But there are a few tips to keep you focused: Take the time to plan your project. Who is the intended recipient and how would you like him or her to feel on receiving the card or tag? What is the purpose of the card? Is it for a special occasion, or simply a "just thinking of you" moment? Learn a few basics about good design and harmonious colors, familiarize yourself with some papers and coloring materials, and not only will you have a much easier time navigating the abundance of available items, you will also be on your way to creating wonderful works of art. And you will have fun.

Mrs. Grossman's Paper Company

Although there are not many rules for good design, it is always a good idea to aim for pleasing rhythm, balanced composition, and harmonious colors. Added embellishments can be as simple as a mat or two of coordinating colors or a torn-paper edge or cut-paper letters. A balanced composiiton will be either symmetrical or asymmetrical. Symmetrical balance is classic and structured, frequently found with centered, formal wedding invitations. Asymmetrical balance is usually less structured and informal. Color elicits definite responses in us. Warm colors—reds and yellows—are stimulating and exciting; cool colors—blues and greens—are calming. A color wheel can always help remind you of how colors work together. But don't forget your intuition. Rely on your own eye to tell you what works. Do *you* like the way specific colors look together? Do *you* find the composition appealing?

We have provided step-by-step instructions for several projects, but the goal of this book is to flood your senses with imaginative techniques for cards, invitations, and gift enclosures. We want to give you ideas, possibilities. You can make the projects exactly as we have, but our hope is that you will take these

Janet Wiliams

projects as inspiration to create your own. Copying every aspect of a project isn't essential, but picking up the spirit of it is. Then you can take the idea and adapt it to your own style and taste. Discover something new for yourself.

Join us in experimenting with paper crafting techniques that range from adding sumptuous color to your projects, (with ink, color pencil, watercolor, embossing, and colored paper); to intriguing folding techniques (including accordion folding, iris folding, and pop-up cards); glorious cut-paper cards and tags; torn paper; punched paper, layered paper; collage; quilling; and ribbon embroidery. Take some time to play with embellishments, those little decorative accents that can make all the difference when you find just the right ones for a special project. Learn to make your own by scanning and creating digital files to use with your crafting.

Paper-craft artists everywhere are exploring ways to create their projects digitally, experimenting with high-tech methods to produce inventive artwork. Inexpensive scanners, computers, software, and printers have made it possible for us to create our own decorative papers and imaginative embellishments, assemble interesting type, manipulate photos, and design imaginative

Susan Swan

layouts. Many crafters working on their computers find that this process has made them more aware of basic graphic design concepts. A scanner lets you copy fragile, old materials or original artwork with freedom to experiment with techniques such as changing or adding color, tearing edges, cropping, and so on—processes that you wouldn't think of trying with original art or special family memorabilia. You can add limitless craft materials to use time and time again by scanning and saving them. Another plus to working on the computer is the freedom to experiment without ruining paper, art, or cardstock. It costs nothing to experiment with a project until you are satisfied with it. Look at the range of possibilities of projects with at least some aspect of digital production, from working with scanned photos, to scanned hand-painted paper, to whole layouts created on the computer. The ideas are limitless, and the production can be a combination of hand- and digital-crafting. Don't forget this amazing tool.

Susan Swan

Whether a simple arrangement of a few elements on a card, or an elaborate presentation, let your imagination speak for you.

Susan Swan

ADDING COLOR

Color is an amazing tool. It generates immediate responses in us. Learn to choose harmonious colors and you will produce appealing cards and tags. Cool colors—blues and greens—are calming while warm colors—reds and yellows—are stimulating. There are any number of techniques to add color to a project— from simple stamping with color added using color pencils, markers, inks, chalks, or watercolor to layered papers, mats, stickers, cut paper, and imaginative embellishments such as ribbons, brads, and flowers.

Bold Garden

Nathalie Métivier, Magenta

MATERIALS

Magenta Rubber stamps:
  Bold Flower and
  Delicate Doodle Branch
White card: 5¼ by 7¼ inch
Cardstock: black, white
Magenta Printed paper:

Victorian Beauty
ColorBox Pigment inkpad:
  Frost White
Prismacolor pencils:
  Chartreuse, Grass
  Green, Light Aqua,

Aquamarine,
Peacock Blue,
White, Indigo Blue

1. Cut the black cardstock into two 3½ by 1½-inch by 2¼-inch piece, Cut white cardstock to 3¾ by 5¾ inches. Stamp the bold flower image three times with Frost White ink on the larger black panel, and the branch on the two smaller panels.

2. Color the bold flower with Aquamarine, Peacock Blue, and Indigo Blue pencils, starting with the darker colors in the center of the flower.

Blend each new, lighter, color into the previous one as you progress to the edges of the flower. Finish with white and Indigo Blue pencils to accent the flower centers. Color the branch with Chartreuse and Grass Green and the buds with Indigo Blue pencil, adding a tiny white dot at each bud center. Edge the green leaves branch with white pencil.

3. Highlight the background around the flowers with the green pencils, starting with the lighter colors, blending each into the previous, darker, shade. Rub with the pencil on its side to "sweep" color on.

4. Attach the branch panels to the outer sides of the white cardstock panel. Center the bold flower panel.

Attach this panel to the back of the printed paper, and the white card.

Bold Flower Variation

Images stamped in white ink on black cardstock offer a dramatic canvas for coloring. The bold flower image dominates each quarter of the square card with a harmonious palette of various blues and greens.

MATERIALS

Magenta Rubber stamp:
  Flower
White card: 5¼" by 5¼"
Black cardstock
Magenta Printed paper:
  Cold Harmony

ColorBox Inkpad: Frost White
Prismacolor pencils:
  Chartreuse, Grass
  Green, Light Aqua,
  Aquamarine, Peacock
  Blue, White, Indigo Blue

Sakura Gelly Roll:
  Stardust
Glossy Accents Lacquer

Nathalie Métivier, Magenta

Cut black cardstock into four 2-inch square tiles. Stamp one flower-shape image in white ink on each black tile. Be sure that the black tiles are on scrap paper so you can stamp some of the image off the edges without damaging your "good" paper. Add color to the stamped images with blue and green color pencils, starting with the darker shades and blending the lighter shades as you add them. Adjust the touch of the pencil to create different weights of color. Outline the colored flower shapes in white pencil to add dimension. Add a dot of Indigo Blue at the center of each flower and circle it with white pencil.

Enhance the background surrounding the flowers with a blue (around the green) or green (around the blue) color pencil on its side. (See Step 3, page 12.) Add a halo of mini dots with the iridescent marker around edges of the green flower petals and at the center of the blue flowers. Add Glossy Accents on the blue flowers.

Layer the four tiles on the printed paper, mat, and card.

Shadowy Dreams

This "ghost stamping" technique presents a gentle, almost-misty scene. All the colors recede. The quiet palette and the silver Peel Off's accent provide just enough texture.

MATERIALS

Magenta Rubber stamps:
   Butterflies Believe
White cardstock
White card: 5¼" by 5¼"
Magenta printed paper:
   Cold Harmony

Silver Peel Off's
ColorBox Pigment Ink Mist
Petal Point: Aqua,
   Peacock
ColorBox white pigment
   ink

Mat knife
Ruler
Cutting board
Adhesive

Cut white cardstock into one panel 3⁵⁄₁₆ by 3¾ inches and one 4¼ by 4¾ inches. Cut the printed paper into one 3½ by 4-inch panel and one 4½ by 5 inches.

Stamp the butterflies pattern on white cardstock with white pigment ink. Starting from the left side, color with Aqua and Peacock ink petals from the Mist Petal Point, blending the two colors as they overlap. Rub off excess ink with a dry paper towel. Stamp the text and swirls with black ink. Cut the stamped image to 3⅛ by 3⁹⁄₁₆ inches. Attach this to the smaller white cardstock and printed paper panesl, and then onto the larger white and printed paper panels.Finlly layer onto the white card.

Finish with silver flourish Peel Off's on the lower right side of the card.

Nathalie Métivier, Magenta

White-embossed Tag

Nathalie Métivier, Magenta

I ridescent inks add a shimmering luxury to a delightful gift tag embellished with soft ribbons. This project is easy and quick, making it possible to create several tags for holiday gifts. The outline image, stamped and embossed in white, resists the color painted on top of it. The white raised outlines are prominent against the black background.

MATERIALS

Magenta Rubber stamp:
   Floral Tag
Cardstock: Black, white
Magenta printed paper:
   Botanical Garden

ColorBox Inkpad:
   Frost White
White embossing
   powder
Heat tool

Duo & Interference
   USArtQuest watercolor
   palette
Green and iridescent
   ribbons

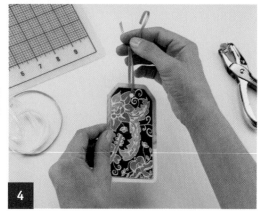

1. Cut black cardstock and white cardstock to 2½ by 4 ¾-inch panels. Cut the printed paper to a 2½ by 3-inch panel. Stamp the Floral Tag image in ColorBox Frost White ink on the black cardstock panel. Emboss with white embossing powder, tapping any excess powder back into its container for future use. Emboss with a heat tool.

2. Paint the flowers with the iridescent inks in the watercolor palette as shown. Use just a small amount of water to apply color evenly and to keep the colors opaque. More water would make the painted image more translucent than we wished. Experiment to see what you prefer.

3. Cut around the tag shape with scissors. Mount the printed paper on the white cardstock panel, aligning the printed paper at the top of the white cardstock. Adhere the stamped, embossed, painted black tag to the printed paper panel.

4. Cut the top corners of the bottom layer at an angle, and round the bottom corners. Punch a small hole at the top of the tag. Add the green ribbon, and finish with several loops of the iridescent ribbon. Add light string to attach the tag to a package, if you wish.

Embossed Enamel Card

Nathalie Métivier, Magenta

Small dollops of clear lacquer add a glistening enamel texture and a hint of dimension to the windblown flowers. Highlighting with a glossy lacquer is a simple way to add dimensional style to a card, and bring the viewer's attention directly to the specific element.

MATERIALS

Magenta rubber stamp:
   3 Flowers
Magenta Cardstock:
   Apple Blossom, Iris,
   white
Magenta printed paper:
   Bubbles
ColorBox Midnight Blue
   pigment ink

Clear Top Boss lacquer
Clear embossing powder
Heat tool
Cat's Eyes pigment ink:
   Sunflower, Orchid,
   Orange
Marvy Markers: Ochre,
   Plum, Pine Green

Prismacolor Pencils:
   Lime Peel, Peacock
   Green, Raspberry,
Black, White
Peel Off's: Turquoise
   Hinges
Peel Off's Markers:
   dark blue

TIP: If the Cat's Eyes ink pads are too wet, as they are sometimes when they are new, use a stylus tool with a white foam tip or a small sponge to apply the ink.

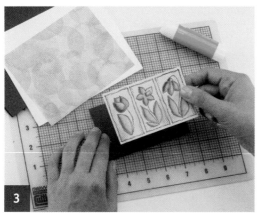

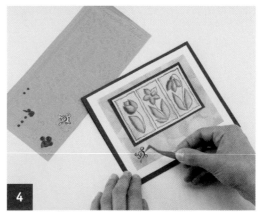

1. Cut the Apple Blossom cardstock to 3½ by 4½ inches. Cut the Iris cardstock to 2¹³⁄₁₆ by 4½ inches. The card is 5½ by 6¾ inches. Cut the white cardstock to a panel measuring 5⅛ by 6⅜ inches. Stamp the image with the Midnight Blue ink on Apple Blossom cardstock and emboss with clear embossing powder. Color with Cat's Eyes Sunflower, Orchid, and Orange ink. Ideally, the Cat's Eyes should not be too wet

2. Color the leaves and flowers with a first coat of faux watercolor made by scribbling waterbase markers on a palette. Paint with a very wet brush and a *little* color to obtain an even paint covering. Enhance the painted flowers and leaves with colored pencils applied with strong quick strokes to create the textured lines. Apply Clear Top Boss to the two outside flower panels. Carefully remove the excess powder around each rectangle. We used a piece of

cardstock to scratch off this excess. Heat set the Clear Top Boss application.

3. Layer the finished panel on the Blue Iris cardstock, then successively onto the printed paper, white cardstock, and the Iris card.

4. Finish by coloring a few Peel Off's turquoise swirls and dots with a dark blue Peel Off's marker, and affixing a few colored dots and swirls to the card as shown.

Simple Color

A touch of color added to a simple stamped image can be perfect. Layer the stamped, colored image onto a mat of harmonious colors to produce a pleasing effect. Start with the darker colors, pressing hard with the pencil and gradually lighten your touch as you move across the image to obtain a smooth gradation in color. Add the lighter shades, overlapping and blending the two colors as you move across the image.

MATERIALS

Memory Box rubber
   stamps: Bee, Cosmos,
   Calendula, Standing
   Santa Bear, Heart
   Balloon

Soft green cards
White cardstock
Mat knife
Ink: Tsukineko VersaFine
   Black

Prismacolor pencils:
   several colors
Scallop punch

Dave Brethauer

Each of the three cards is stamped in black ink on white cardstock and then colored with beautifully blended colored pencil. The application of color to these stamped images is a fine guide to selecting harmonious and appropriate colors for your palette. Starting with the bear's hat in the card at the left, the green dots on the red party hat demonstrate the use of complementary colors—complementary colors red and green are opposite one another on the color wheel. The green wheelbarrow filled with blue blossoms uses two analogous colors (adjacent colors on the color wheel), and the gate card at the bottom again uses complementary colors of orange and blue in the flower blooms.

On Wings of Flight

The dramatic dark solid-shape bird stamped in Chocolate brown over the Turquoise Gem and Tea Leaves flourishes produces an eye-catching composition in an engaging palette.

MATERIALS

Memory Box Rubber stamps: Resting Bird, Early Bird, Classic Flourish, Verdi Flourish, Bird Branch, flower

Memory Box Paper: Eggshell, Robin's Egg, Vanilla Bean
Robin's Egg card
Tsukineko VersaMagic

Ink: Gingerbread, Turquoise Gem, Sea Breeze, Tea Leaves
Tsukineko Brilliance ink: Chocolate

For the card at the back, stamp the flourishes in Tea Leaves and Turquoise VersaMagic and small round flowers in Sea Breeze on Eggshell cardstock. Stamp the Resting Bird image in the center of the central flourish in Brilliance Chocolate ink.

Run the Gingerbread Versa Magic ink pad quickly around the edges of the stamped cardstock to create a soft, vintage look.

Adhere the stamped panel to a Vanilla Bean mat slightly larger than the panel and then to the Robin's Egg card.

Irene Seifer from a concept by Dave Brethauer

21

Fanciful Folio

A timeless springtime image with an old-world sensibility provides a handsome cover for a memory-filled collection of timeless family photographs. The spring season, time for rebirth and growth, provides a thoughtful background for the vintage photos.

MATERIALS

Memory Box Rubber stamps: Early Bird, Classic Flourish, Verdi Flourish, Bird Branch, flower
Memory Box Paper: Eggshell, Robin's Egg, Vanilla Bean
Robin's Egg card
Tsukineko VersaMagic Ink: Gingerbread, Turquoise Gem, Sea Breeze, Tea Leaves
Tsukineko Brilliance ink: Pearlescent Chocolate
Ribbon: May Arts

Stamp the branches, flowers, and flourish in the VersaMagic inks and stamp the solid early bird in chocolate Brilliance ink atop the Tea Leaves branches. Add the Turquoise flourish and Sea Breeze flowers. Ink the sides of the Eggshell card to create the "distressed" edges, and layer onto the Vanilla Bean and Robin's Egg cardstock mats.

Use the template on page 109 to create the folio. The simple folding starts with a 12 by 12 inch cardstock sheet and is folded in half vertically and horizontally, creasing and unfolding each time, and then each of the lower corners is folded diagonally to the center point. The folio can hold photographs, gift certificates, tickets, and many other favorite items.

Layer a generous length of double-sided ribbon under the Robin's Egg mat and adhere the matted stamped panel to the Eggshell card. Tie a bow with the ribbon at the right side of the card to hold the folio closed.

Irene Seifer from concept by Dave Brethauer

Translucent Sticker Color

Bright translucent stickers are a delightful and easy way to add color to cards and tags. The display of colorful balloons, stars, and bubbles on these invitations look spontaneous, cheerful, and fun.

MATERIALS

Mrs. Grossman's card stock in various colors
White cardstock
Mrs. Grossman's acetate stickers: stars,
balloons, bubbles
Ribbons: various
Brads
Wire clips
Computer and printer

Mrs. Grossman's Paper Company

Create the invitation text on your computer and print it on white cardstock. Trim to an appropriate size.

Decorate the printed invitation panel with the colorful acetate stickers. Create a sense of movement by extending some stickers off the panel edges and trim off the excess with scissors. Attach the printed, decorated panel to bright-colored cardstock with colored brads, wire clips, or glue. Embellish with colorful ribbons as shown. Note that a mat with extra space at the top allows space for embellishing with ribbons and other materials.

Cut Paper

This delightful cut-paper technique offers an imaginative way to add color to cards and tags. The exciting palette offers a powerful presentation for the simple designs.

MATERIALS

Various color papers

3 different size hole punches

Background paper with black polka dots on a red base sets the tone. We offer two versions for the covering layer—one black and one white. The effect of the two colors is quite different.

The letters are created with brilliant-colored hand-painted papers, scanned and printed. The artist cut and assembled the simple letter forms. Create these papers with paint on white paper. Scan the papers, print them, and cut the letterforms and decorative rule. Punch three differ-

ent-sized holes in the card. Create the type on a computer and print it on card-

stock. Layer the colorful collage-like panel over the red-and-black polka-dot base.

Susan Swan

25

FOLDING

There is something marvelously appealing about the added dimension of folded projects. The texture and weight in the folded segments, elements that unwind as you open a card, or the excitement of the secret not-yet-known for cards that pop up or out when you open the card appeal to one's imagination and sense of joy.

Folded Album Card

Avery simple accordion-folded card with four colorful panels is just right to celebrate a lovely young girl's birthday. The card is meant to stand upright as a long-term memento of the special day.

MATERIALS

Cardstock: red, green, yellow, bright pink, orange
Mrs. Grossman's Stickers:

Sparkle Confetti, Party Tickets
Silver Gelly Roll pen

Mini envelopes
Photographs or computer and printer

Mrs. Grossman's Paper Company

Mount yellow and hot pink panels to two of the pages. Mat photographs on contrasting color cardstock and attach to the card. Add mini envelopes layered with tickets and embellish with Sparkle Confetti stickers as shown.

Accordion-fold the finished card into four pages, with a valley fold at center and mountain folds between the remaining panels.

Cut red cardstock to a panel measuring 9 by 4 inches and green cardstock to measure 6 by 4 inches. Form the card base by layering the green cardstock over the red, overlapping one panel.

28

Accordion Grandpa

arm colors exude the warmth felt for this Grandpa. Naptime on his day seems like a very good idea. It's time to join in! Three favorite photographs of Grandpa are mounted on the layered background paper in a loose free-form design, one overlapping the other.

MATERIALS

Printed papers: hand-painted light peach and orange, red polka-dot, tan

Photographs or computer and printer
Red polka-dot stickers

A pretty printed paper with delicate burnt orange swirls on a light peach background stretches across the width of the three-paneled card. Two layers of handmade paper painted in a soft, textured tan color are torn and layered on the printed paper background.

The photographs of Grandpa have been printed from the computer, decorated with a message to Grandpa and two cheery red hearts, layered onto a red polka-dot mat and then a torn hand-painted paper mat. A signature completes the picture.

Accordion-fold the card horizontally in thirds, with the first fold a mountain fold and the second a valley fold.

Susan Swan

Shaped Panel Card

Nathalie Métivier, Magenta

A unique envelope-style card relies on gently shaded color, simple cutting, and easy folding to make a lovely impression. Two folds divide the card into three vertical sections. The bottom panel folds up, the top one folds down and attaches to the bottom panel with ribbon wrapped around a brad. A silhouetted stamped flower embellishes the top panel.

TIP: To prevent tearing, try punching a small hole with a needle or awl before inserting a brad in delicate paper.

MATERIALS

Magenta Rubber stamps:
  Panel stamp, Flowers,
  Single flower
Ivory cardstock
Magenta printed paper:
  Botanical Garden

Colorbox Fluid Chalk inkpad:
  Dark Moss
Prismacolor pencils:
  Bronze, Olive Green,
  White, Black, Imperial

Violet, Parma Violet,
  Lavender, Orange
Ribbon: violet
Brads: 2 mini orange

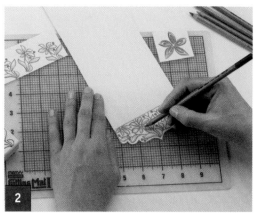

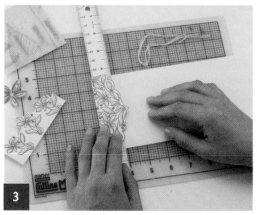

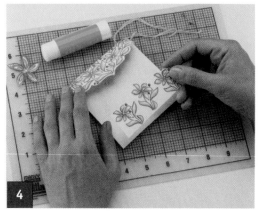

1. Cut three pieces of ivory cardstock: one to 4¼ by 10 inches, one to 4 by 1¾ inches and one to 1¾-inch square. Using Dark Moss Fluid Chalk ink stamp the panel image at the bottom of the large cardstock panel, the row of flowers on the medium panel, and the single flower on the small panel. Cut the printed paper to 3¼ by 3½-inches.

2. Trim the 4¼-inch stamped cardstock panel to a width of

4 inches, flush on each side of the stamped image. Silhouette the shaped panel edge. Color the images with colored pencils.

3. Rotate the card clockwise and score a fold line just past the stamped image straight edge, and fold the card. Fold the bottom edge of the card up to meet the top one. Cut loosely around the top edge of the row of flowers. Silhouette the single flower image.

4. Attach the printed paper panel at the bottom fold line. Attach the three flowers along the bottom fold of the card over the printed paper.

Carefully insert a brad through the center of the bottom middle flower. Insert a brad through the center of the single flower and the tip of the shaped panel at the top of the card. Attach the ribbon to the brad.

Envelope card

An elegant, very simple folded envelope card of the softest ivory is dressed to the nines with a stamped and quilled medallion and gold edging applied with a metallic gold pen. The basic "under/over" closing fold for the envelope is one that many of us learned as children. See the template on page 109. This makes a lovely gift tag or table place card.

Janet Williams

32

Baby Announcement Envelope

A small one-piece card-and-envelope-in-one is perfect when the written message is not too long. This elegant baby announcement uses a card/envelope with an additional layered panel that sits inside the folded envelope. The artwork is created with stickers on vellum layered on cardstock with type on the lower level. See the template on page 109.

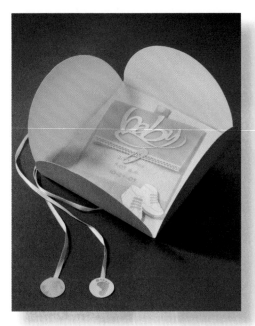

Mrs. Grossman's Paper Company

MATERIALS

Template for the card/
  envelope shape
Vellum: aqua

Cardstock: aqua, yellow
Mrs. Grossman's stickers:
Baby Milestones, Baby Paper

Whispers
Ribbon: narrow
Computer and printer

Baby Announcement Card

Bright, clean, joyous colors send a cele-bratory message with cards announcing the birth of a baby. This triple-panel card features a gorgeous baby peeking out from two square windows cut at different sizes and angles. The layering of the heart stickers with foam dots adds dimension.

The window card starts with a rectangular piece of card-stock that is folded horizon-tally in thirds, first from the right side to center and then from the left side to the far edge of the first folded panel, overlapping the first panel. The square windows cut into the top two card lay-ers are at right angles to each other, with the second one smaller and fitting right in-side the first window creating an interesting frame-within-a-frame for the photograph attached to the base (center) section of the card. Charming stickers embellish the card. Save a digital photograph on a computer in Photoshop and then create a layout on the computer and position the photograph on the page with the type, producing a single printed sheet. Or attach the photograph to the page with the type in place.

MATERIALS

Cardstock: pink, white
Stickers: Simply Sassy

Elephants, Folk Hearts
Foam Dots

Horizontal-fold Window Card

Fun with color and shapes brings smiles. A bold, sunshine-filled palette sets a warm tone for a beach-party invitation. The shaped windows provide texture and charming dimension, allowing for the placement of smile-producing stickers back-to-back overlapping the windows bringing a finished look to the windows front and back when you open the card. Who could resist palm trees, starfish, beach chairs, pails, and shovels?

MATERIALS NEEDED

One 12-inch square
  of cardstock: yellow
Stickers: Simply Sassy Beach
  Chairs, Pail & Shovel,

Island Palm Tree,
  Tags Red and
  Yellow, Small Tags
Brad

Glue
Type (hand-written or
  computer composed
  and printed)

This distinctive two-fold card starts with a 12-inch square of cardstock. Measure and mark the card into three equal vertical segments. Fold the bottom edge of the cardstock up one-third of the height of the sheet. Crease and maintain this fold. Then fold the top edge of the cardstock down over the first fold to align at the bottom edge of the first fold, now the bottom edge of the card. You now have three panels.

Once you have created the folds, determine where you will cut the two windows so they will overlap. Cut or punch a square window in the top panel on the left side of the card. Cut or punch another window, smaller than the first so that it sits inside the first one, and rotated 45 degrees in the middle panel just behind the front one.

The invitation information is on the bottom panel. Embellish

the window edges with back-to-back beach-chair and palm-tree stickers.

Wrap the card with a decorated band of yellow cardstock. Finish the band with a double-layer tag decorated with a starfish sticker. Attach the tag to the wrapped band with a brad. We have presented additional decorative party tabletop items—two place card/party favors with small tags and stickers.

BEACH PARTY!

Pop-up Cards

Susan Swan

The idea of creating pop-up cards may seem a little out-of-one's league. But really, they do not have to be difficult to produce. A little planning is necessary, but the pop-up mechanics are easy. Try it, and have fun.

Here are two great holiday pop-up cards. There are many ways to create these projects. The artist hand-painted the orange paper on the front and scanned it into her computer and then printed and trimmed it. The word "JOY" was cut from another sheet of the same printed paper. On the one card, the letters are layered on a scanned and printed collaged

MATERIALS

Photos
Paper: hand-painted, or

special wrapping
    paper, or wall paper

we wish you
peace and love
this holiday season

Susan Swan

music score, cut with a lacy edge and mounted on the pop-up brace. The second card features a photograph "adjusted" in Photoshop as the background and the word "JOY" silhouetted leaving the space in the center of the "O" intact; that section is used to attach the word to the pop-up brace. See the template on page 110. The center folds for the pop-up construction are horizontal.

Use these ideas to inspire your own versions of pop-up cards. Try a photo of a favorite scene, or your own artwork. The steps are easy, and they produce one-of-a-kind cards.

Winter Trees Pop-up

Two stunning winter scenes bring us right into the Robert Frost poem "Stopping by Woods on a Snowy Evening." The snowy early-evening color of the cover releases to an interior winter-black sky of night with snow drifts and blanketed tree branches. The focal point is a decorated Christmas tree and holiday greeting against a multi-colored mini-star-strewn sky that we see in the distance through a large evergreen-shape die-cut window.

These papers are painted, but beautiful wrapping paper, printed papers, photographs, or your own painted scenes would be effective.

For the top layer—the window card—fold and score cardstock (9¾ by 5 inches) in quarters. The middle score line is the center fold of the cut-out window. Use the template on page 110 to cut out the tree-shape window at the middle score line. Fold on each of the scored lines—a mountain fold at center and valley folds on the lines at each side of the cut shape. Fold and score another piece of same-size cardstock. Decorate it as you wish for the "background" scene. Valley fold the center of this card. Glue the far left rectangle of the window "cut-out" card to the left edge of the "background" card. Repeat the process with the right side of the cards.

Susan Swan

Holiday Pop-Up Card

Susan Swan. Family photo by Rebecca Cawley.

Pop-up cards are guaranteed to deliver delight and pleasure. This holiday pop-up is full of warm family sensibilities from a beckoning bright red door with a wreath and ribbon, to a porch rocking chair, assorted newspaper lines, and a once-gingham fabric roof, not to mention the Christmas-carol music background.

This cheerful pop-up card started with a cut-paper collage made of scanned fabric, music sheets, cardboard, and various other papers. The collage was assembled in Photoshop, printed on white cardstock, and then folded and glued into the pop-up card as shown. A good family photo is important. A colorful background was provided for this digital photo in Photoshop and then it was printed on white cardstock. The card actually consists of three layers: the card itself with the photo printed on it, the pop-up window, and the cover.

Pop-up Announcement

A cheerful pop-up card is a great idea for a birth announcement, especially when the new baby is not the first-born so all the little sibling ducks in a row can show their pleasure! "Everyone is just Ducky" and all seem poised, ready to quack for the newest little one. The bright palette is simple and effective, presenting the pop-up feature beautifully.

MATERIALS

Card: Mrs. Grossman's
Stickers: Mrs. Grossman's
  Simply Sassy Ducks

Cardstock: white, pale yellow
Foam Dots
Text panel

The card is a Simply Sassy pop-up card from Mrs. Grossman's.

Layer the duck sticker on white and attach to the front of the card.

Create the text on a computer and print it on pale yellow cardstock. Trim and attach it to the bottom of the white cardstock panel.

Pinch the pop-up folds to help them stand at right angles to the card. Attach four baby ducks with the two in the back row facing in one direction and the two in the front row facing in the opposite direction. Attach the mother duck. Powder the back of the stickers that extend beyond the pop-up braces to prevent them from sticking to the card when it is closed.

Mrs. Grossman's Paper Company

Boxed Invitation

It's fun to create a package with unexpected elements. Here we have a New Year's Eve party invitation in a handmade folded box. We wanted to hand deliver the invitations in their own special package.

MATERIALS

Cardstock: gray heavy weight, black
Decorative-edge scissors
Hole punch or awl

Metallic thread: silver, gold
Star stickers (or star punch and metallic papers)

Computer-generated type (or pen for hand-written information)

Mrs. Grossman's Paper Company

Cut gray cardstock to a tag shape measuring 2¼ by 5 inches. Cut a second gray cardstock panel 2 by 4 inches. Cut a third gray cardstock piece approximately 6½ by 2 inches (long enough to wrap around the three-sided box with enough to tuck under the wrap). Cut a black cardstock panel 2⅛ by 4⅛ inches. Trim the black cardstock panel with decorative-edge scissors.

Create type on a computer or handwrite the invitation on the small gray cardstock panel. Embellish the panel with stickers. Mount the type panel onto the deckle-edged

black cardstock panel. Punch five holes along a short edge of the gray tag. Center the mounted type panel on the remaining space of the gray tag. Embellish the tag by threading metallic cord through the punched holes and completing with back-to-back star stickers at the cord ends. Placing two stickers back-to-back allows a "finished" view front and back.

Wrap the finished box with the strip of gray cardstock, and wrap the panel with metallic cord embellished with multi back-to-back star stickers.

Asian Star Tea-bag Folding

Originating in the Netherlands, tea-bag folding consists of folding shapes from small squares of paper to assemble in a dimensional motif. This wheel-like arrangement of red and gold diamond-shaped petals is anchored with a gold good-luck charm at its center. An elegant, controlled palette, strong geometric shapes (circles, squares, triangles/diamonds) and a classic symmetrical design contribute to a pleasing, harmonious presentation.

The palette for this project is strong and unifying. The three papers—one crinkled metallic gold, one red and gold, and one red, gold, and white— repeat the colors of the mats and large circular window through which we see the artful arrangement of folded papers. Fold a total of fifteen Diamond Fold tea-bag shapes, five with each of the three papers, following the folding instructions on page 106.

Arrange the folded diamonds in an overlapping circle on a white textured cardstock panel. Mat the panel with crinkled metallic gold and mount on the white card. Add a red square frame with a circular window cut to barely clear the outer edge of the circle of folded diamonds. Anchor the center of the folded circle with a gold Asian Happiness coin.

Irene Seifer

Rosette Tea-bag Fold

A palette of strong pink and purple will capture one's attention! Choose printed paper with your palette in mind, or stamp a selected solid paper with a pattern in a harmonious ink color. The interlocking shapes of the tea-bag folded squares create a dimensional motif.

Irene Seifer

An assortment of various harmonious ribbons anchors the tea-bag-folded rosette ornament to the card. Small gems accent the folded shapes.

Follow the drawings for the Star Square fold on page 107. Make eight Star Square folds and arrange them in an interlocking circle to form the rosette shape. Add small glass gems at the point of each folded shape, and one at the center of the rosette, Fold several different-patterned ribbon lengths in half to tuck under the featured rosette and cascade down the front of the card.

Iris-folded Rainy Day

Iris folding originated in the Netherlands (as did tea-bag folding). Its similarity to the iris of an eye or camera inspired the name. Narrow strips of several different color papers are folded and arranged in a spiral pattern with a central opening, creating a center eye with shutter-like layers. The illusion of depth is striking.

MATERIALS

Cardstock: brown, turquoise, aqua
Ribbon: blue-and-white stripe, aqua, 2 brown
and turquoise
Die-cut umbrella template

Make a copy of the iris-folding pattern on page 108. Cut an opening the same size as the overall pattern in a piece of cardstock. Tape the cardstock, right-side down, on top of the pattern so the pattern shows through the window. There are five layers. Each layer of the project has one each of the four ribbons. Divide the ribons into piles labeled A, B, C, D. Select one from each pile to lay on the pattern as marked—1A, 1B, 1C, 1D followed by 2A, 2B etc. Remove the design from the pattern and turn over the the card-stock. Mount the framed design directly on a card or decorative paper. This iris-folded design is layered

Irene Seifer

with a commercial die-cut umbrella window template. A cheerful bow of the blue-and-white ribbon is tied on the handle cut from rich brown cardstock.The scattered raindrops add a final touch.

Iris-folded Christmas Tree

A variation on the usual folded-paper iris-folded projects is offered here without any folded paper, but with red and green ribbons forming the iris platform. Iris-folding started with folding narrow strips of paper layered in a spiral pattern. The folding added dimension. The ribbons used in this iris arrangement are grosgrain and have some dimension. The gingham bow is made from a lighter-weight polyester ribbon.

MATERIALS

Cardstock: white, red, green
Ribbon: 4 red and green patterns

Christmas tree template
Rubber stamp: holly leaves
Glossy Accent

Irene Seifer

Use the iris-folding template on page 108. A white cardstock commercial die-cut Christmas-tree shape is layered over the Christmasy red-and-green iris base. The palette is simple and is reinforced with each design component. The red and green ribbons are complemented by the red and green mats and the red and green holly border running down the right side of the card. Glossy accents embellish each holly leaf and berry.

Elegant Iris Fold

The striking, sophisticated palette of gold and black sets the tone for a special, formal occasion. The palette is uncomplicated, the geometric shapes are simple, and the symmetrical composition is strong. The widened iris pattern heightens the feeling of motion.

MATERIALS

Cardstock: gold, black
Paper: various black and gold

A simple rectangle provides the frame for the iris-folded image. A triangle of the paper used at the center of the iris-fold provides a stunning roof over the top of the image. The layers of folded paper create extraordinary texture and depth. The template on page 108 has five layers; add one more to it.

Irene Seifer

Cut two strips of each of the four papers about ¾ inch wide and 10 inches long. Separate the patterns into four piles, and label them A to D. Fold a narrow hem from the front to back side of the paper along the length of each paper strip. Remember that you will be working from the back of the card. When finished you will turn over the completed pattern. Each layer consists of one paper from each pattern. Lay one strip from pile A face down with the folded edge toward the center of the pattern on the template area marked 1A. Trim the strip leaving about ¼ inch of the strip off each end of the segment of the pattern. Glue or tape the paper strip down. Follow with a strip from B onto 1B, then C, and then D in the same way. Proceed with the subsequent strips in this alternating pattern.

CUTTING, TEARIN

G AND PUNCHING

Who can resist cutting paper? And coloring the paper before cutting it adds to the delight. We have included projects with the paper cut into small bits, assembled, and used to construct a new form; we have projects in which we have made a simple cut to release a surprise in the original shape; and we have included projects where we have cut the paper into a new shape altogether. But cutting paper is not the only way to alter paper. Tearing paper carefully releases a sumptuous soft edge as a stunning design element. Punching shapes and adhering them to a card can produce magical results.

Cut-paper Happy Birthday

Various painted papers are used to create playful letters and a flower on a delightful birthday card and envelope. The letters and flowers are layered onto shiny black paper. The front of the card is cut smaller to reveal the flower at the right edge of the interior page.

MATERIALS

Papers: many colors and patterns, purchased or created with paint, ink, or chalk

Cardstock: White, black, red/orange, orange

Punch: Circle, flower blossom

There are various ways to produce this card. We hope you will take the ideas we present and find your way to produce them. Cut a selection of brilliant papers into manageable sizes. Assemble various snippets of the cut paper shapes to create letters to spell the message "Happy Birthday."

Or paint several sheets of smooth watercolor (hot press) paper with your own palette and designs. Scan the papers to keep so you have them for future use, print them out and cut the printed papers. Or cut the originals. However you choose, you will assemble the cut papers into letterforms to create the message. Susan scanned her hand-painted art, printed it, and cut the printed papers. She then has them to use for other projects, or for when she wants to make multiple copies of a card.

Susan Swan

Cut Birthday Candles

celebratory palette, a symmetrical design, and imaginative components offer an intriguing project. The giant birthday candles are imaginative. Everything angles to the center—a visually-appealing strong symmetrical arrangement. The semi-circle window cut in the top front of this cheerful card allows us to see through to an arc of yellow stars against a black background on the interior page. When the card is opened those stars are revealed to be lit candles, the flames being the stars and the candles themselves tall, angled strips of painted pink paper stretching to the stars. The original paper was hand-painted and scanned. The cutting was done on the computer in Photoshop, as was the type, the irregular edge at the top and sides. One could create this project by hand—painted papers and scanned or not for cutting. But digital work is exciting and economical.

Susan Swan

Christmas Cut-out

The simplicity of this design makes it disarming. Holiday colors, playful edging, and a hint of something we can't quite see teases us with anticipation. The slightly angled cut edge at the fold of the card gives us no indication of what's to come on the interior. When opened, the secretive cut becomes a Christmas tree—the cut half-image on the double-layer, folded, card opens to be a full tree cut into the center fold of the card. The artist added a free-form gold star at the top of the tree with decorative ornaments and snow drifting down each side. The unexpected pinkish-purple greeting embellishes the palette.

This card was created on a computer in Photoshop.

Susan Swan

Valentine Heart Cut-out

Hand-painted paper in blue-green and tan, text layered onto a blue panel, scanned lace bordering the edge of the card were all assembled on the computer. The cutting detail is simple: the card front is cut about ½ inch narrower than the interior leaf so the lace border peeks out. The hook shape cut into both layers at the fold reveals itself to be a whole heart when the card is opened. How many of us spent hours cutting such shapes out of folded paper as children?

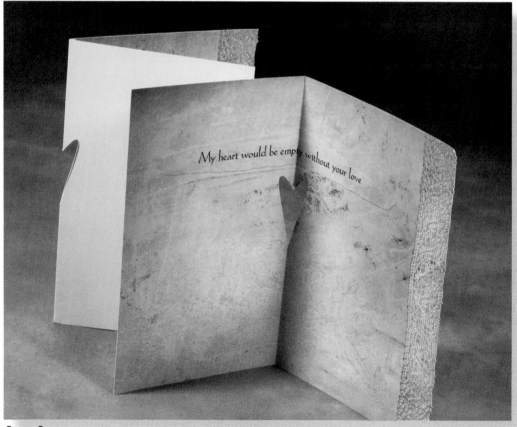

My heart would be empty without your love

Susan Swan

Halloween Cut-out

A pumpkin-colored smiling cut-out profile with a bat-in-flight eye has to make you smile. Open the card and a giant orange and blue squiggly pumpkin stares back at us. The bats are now inserted into yellow triangle eyes and the "Happy Halloween" message looks like a jumbled, zany assortment of newspaper letters. The half-mouth and nose cut into the folded card expands to the full face on the inside of the card.

The paper for the interior pumpkin is paste paper created by the artist and scanned into the computer. Paste paper is a textured paper you can make at home. An acrylic-paste mixture is brushed onto heavy paper (like Canson Mi-Tiente) and scraped to show the paper underneath. One can create scalloped, wavy, or straight lines by pulling combs or other tools across the paste-covered sheets. Overlapped patterns create a three-dimensional effect. The technique has been used for bookmaking and mixed media work for centuries. There are various recipes using wallpaper paste or flour, etc. You can find more

Susan Swan

information, recipes, and examples of paste-paper online at www.rubber-stampsclub.com/tips/papermaking.

Cut-paper Caricatures

The whole card is cut into a humorous, exaggerated personal profile with imaginative details, like garden-plant hair for the gardener, a band-aid for Mr. Fix-it etc. The idea is to choose a characteristic of the person (the recipient) and emphasize that—perhaps an ever-present hat or splotches of dust or paint on the handyman-around-the-house; or the shock of hair on Dad's head; or the cap and hair on a niece's head; or the eagle eye of Grandma gardener. The point is to have lighthearted fun.

One of our favorite techniques is to add dimensional embellishments to the digitally constructed cards, like the brass eye sprocket, the band-aid, the cut- printed paper hair and the fabric flower on gardening Grandma.

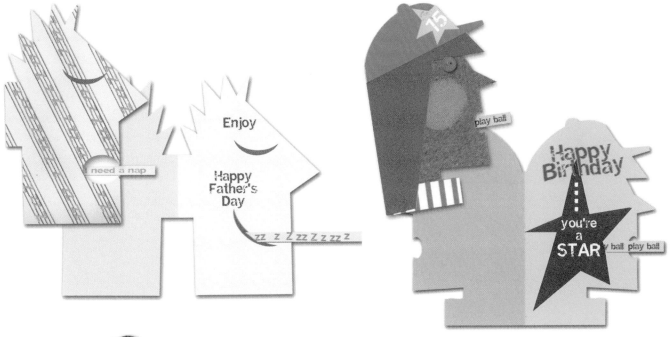

need a nap

Enjoy

Happy
Father's
Day

zz z Z zz Z z zz z

15

play ball

Happy
Birthday

you're
a
STAR

play ball play ball

The "Need a nap" card has a tag suggesting the nap to be pulled out when the card is opened. Create everything on the computer and assemble with real elements, or create a collage with available papers by hand and add dimensional embellishments.

I need compost

There's nothing like
a birthday in spring
for my favorite
green thumb
...
enjoy!

Susan Swan

Torn-paper Trilogy

Paper tears beautifully. A torn edge is easy to accomplish and is one of the most effective dimensional elements. A small tag with a soft palette and a gently torn edge seems very appropriate for a baby announcement. Add two more tags with beautiful baby photos and attach them all together with a brad and a delicate apricot ribbon rose and you have something special.

MATERIALS

Ivory cardstock
Jo Sonja acrylic paint:
   Cadmium Orange
Ribbons: Narrow

decorative ribbons
Computer font: Adobe EVA
Brad
Photographs: scanned

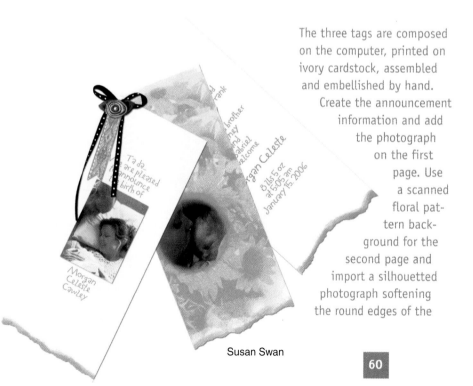

Susan Swan

The three tags are composed on the computer, printed on ivory cardstock, assembled and embellished by hand. Create the announcement information and add the photograph on the first page. Use a scanned floral pattern background for the second page and import a silhouetted photograph softening the round edges of the photo in Photoshop; add type to the last page. Print the three pages in a peach-orange color, and trim to the appropriate size. Tear the bottom edge of each page and lightly brush Cadmium Orange acrylic paint over the edges of all three tags.

Experiment with colors and coloring agents of your own choosing.

Torn Painted-paper Card

Hand-painted paper, a garden photograph, handmade photo corners and several other elements make this thoughtful card a gift to treasure. Seeds enclosed in the small handmade envelope are for the recipient to plant and tend, guaranteeing they will remember the gift for a long time.

MATERIALS

Cardstock: white, yellow
Vellum
Garden photo
Canson Mi-Teintes paper

Checkerboard paper
Computer type
Envelope clasps with
    string

Eyelets
Eyelet tool
White paint

Hand-paint the paper in soft tones of green with streaks of brown. Or find an appealing, garden-like paper. Fold a 5 by 6½-inch card from the painted paper. Cut photo corners from a checkerboard pattern paper and layer over the four corners of the garden photograph. Add a small mesage panel along the top of the photo.

Add a small vellum panel with planting instructions printed in white to the interior right side of the card. Make a small packet for the seeds with the yellow cardstock and checkerboard paper. Add seeds from a

Susan Swan

nursery or your own garden into the packet, attach the clasps, close the envelope, and attach it to the card below the vellum panel. Tear

the hand-painted paper card front down the right side. Brush the torn edge with white acrylic paint for added emphasis.

Soft-edge Card

An elegant palette, a contrasting undulating edge, and a laser-cut medallion with narrow textured ribbons cascading from it's center create a stunning effect.

MATERIALS

Cards: Mrs. Grossman's
   Twilight and Licorice cards
Cardstock: Black

Stickers: Filligree Medallions
Ribbons
Tiny glass beads

Foam adhesive strips

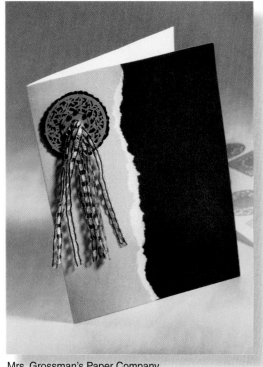

Mrs. Grossman's Paper Company

Tear the Twilight card down the middle of the front, creating a significant undulating line. Remove the right-hand section of the card. Layer the torn Twilight card over a Licorice card front.

Mount a filigree medallion sticker on a slightly larger black cardstock circle cut with a delicate decorative edge. Add eight black tiny glass gems. Fold several 7½-inch ribbons in half to approximately 3¾-inch strips. Position (but do not attach yet) the mounted medallion in the upper left area of the Twilight card to determine the placement of two small holes to be punched in the cardstock beneath the medallion center. Punch the two small holes and thread the ribbons in one hole and out the other. Punch a hole in the medallion center, add eight small black glass gems outlining the center circle of the medallion, and mount the decorated medallion on the card with foam adhesive strips. Pull the ribbons through the hole punched in the medallion center to let them cascade down the front of the card.

Torn-paper Christmas Card

The geometry of a very precise, rectangular panel with images of very precise triangular Christmas trees is beautifully balanced by a generous torn-edge wave of white in a sea of yellow and gold highlighted with Christmas reds and greens. A patterned paper extension of matte gold metallic paper decorated with the small Fun Christmas Tree ornament stickers complements the angular trees with the same palette. Playing with shapes and colors offers great enjoyment.

Mrs. Grossman's Paper Company

MATERIALS

Cards: Mrs. Grossman's Just Plain Vanilla Studio Card
Paper: Matte gold metallic

Stickers: Mrs. Grossman's Fun Christmas Trees
Foam panels

Punch a Posy

If ever there was an economic paper-crafting tool, it is the hand-held paper punch. With one punch you can create many projects using both the positive and negative punched shapes. Layering the punched shapes adds texture and dimension. Experiment with a few punches and various papers, and have fun.

MATERIALS

Punches: vase, branches, flower, small circle
Cardstock: 2 shades of pink, shades of brown, gray swirl
Ribbon

Judy Ritchie

The palette is simple and consistent. Create the punched collage image first. Punch the vase from the gray swirl cardstock, followed by the branches. Then punch the three flowers in pink (two light pink and one darker). Finally punch one small circle out of brown cardstock and two from the gray swirl. Attach the vase to the center of the bottom section of a brown cardstock panel, layer the branches so they arch out of the vase, and add the three flowers and their small punched circle centers. Mat the featured decorated panel on slightly lighter brown cardstock, and then attach this matted panel to the pink card. Embellish the base with a tiny bow of pink ribbon.

TIP: Tweezers are a great help in placing small or delicate items on a project like the branches on this card.

Punched Mother's Day Card

The palette is effective—warm brown and pink; the centered composition is pleasing, but the most interesting aspect of this card is the double-layered punched flower with soft textured ribbon wrapping through its petals. The two punched flowers are arranged so that the petals of one layer alternate with the petals of the other.

MATERIALS

Punch: large flower, corner punch
Rubber stamp: Flower stem, Happy Mother's
Day
Ribbon
Cardstock: white, light pink, dark pink, mocha brown
Ink: green, black
Colored pencil: Lyra green

Punch two flowers from the light pink cardstock. Cut a white cardstock panel to 2½ by 4¹³⁄₁₆ inches. Stamp the flower stem in green ink at the center bottom of the white cardstock panel and shade the edges with green colored pencil. Mount one punched flower on the white cardstock panel just above the stem. Wind pink ribbon between each petal of a second flower as shown and layer it on top of the first, rotating the top flower so that the petals are in an alternate pattern.

Stamp the Mother's Day greeting. Round the corners of the featured panel. Layer it onto a slightly larger mat of pink cardstock with rounded corners, and then onto a mocha brown panel cut slightly smaller than the white card. Adhere the multi layers to the white card front. For added effect, gently lift the individual petals off the page.

Judy Ritchie

Punched and Embellished Card

You don't need a lot of punches to create interesting projects. Playing with color adds interest and dimension to a project. Narrow sparkling ribbon winds around the petals of a soft lavender punched flower that is layered over a darker violet flower. Color, texture, and shape play together to capture our attention.

MATERIALS

Cardstock: White, mocha brown, lavender, violet
Printed paper: Multi-colored stripe

Rubber stamp:
ColorBox Pigment inkpad: Green, Brown
Color pencils: Lyra Soft

Green
Sparkle: Stickles
Glass Gems
Ribbon: Glitter

Judy Ritchie

Layer multi-colored striped paper onto a white card with the fold at the top of the card—an easel fold, leaving a narrow white border. Stamp the floral image on the upper left portion of a small white cardstock panel. Stamp the message in the lower right corner of the same panel. Punch two flowers, one from violet cardstock and one from lavender cardstock. Wrap the glittery cord around the petals of the lavender flower as shown, and layer it on the darker punched flower. Add a glass gem at the center of the top flower and attach the layered flowers to the white panel overlapping the stamped greenery as shown. Add three glass gems to the lower right corner of the panel. Mount the decorated panel with a mocha brown mat and mount this onto the striped paper layer on the white card.

Dimensional Bouquet

A fresh arrangement of always-lovely daisies graces a leaf-strewn card. A sparkling, clean palette, a centered arrangement, and textured layers provide effective and pleasing dimension.

MATERIALS

Cardstock: dark green, yellow checkerboard, yellow, white

Punches: Large daisy, small daisy, tiny flower, mini flower, leaf, corner punch

Glass gems

The appeal of layered images or components in a pleasing composition is a given: Dimension is intriguing. The yellow field filled with dark green leaves and finished with white daisies with yellow flower-shaped centers pleases on many levels. Gently lift the punched daisy petals from the surface and you add further interest. The card is simple, and much of the fun is in the layering of the daisy shapes. Punch eight leaves out of green cardstock and arrange them in a loose pattern on a yellow checkerboard cardstock panel. Punch two of each-sized daisy shapes to create each of the three large and two small flowers. Punch the yellow center shapes. Layer two same-size punched daisies, rotating the top one so that the petals alternate rather than align to make the flower look full. Add the punched yellow centers, and then the glass gems. Mount the daisies on the leaf-strewn panel. Round the corners with the corner punch and layer onto a white rounded-corner mat. Adhere the layered panel to the green card.

Irene Seifer

LAYERING

AND COLLAGE

Paper is so amenable. We have seen how it folds, bends, cuts, and tears. And now dramatic three-dimensional layering of one paper over another creates intriguing depth and composition. One element on a page can be stunning. But layer one element on another, and you create something very appealing. Layer several elements and you have something extraordinary.

White-embossed Layers

The simple arrangement of this soft card elicits a calm response in us. The faux watercolor palette of summertime green, white, and pink is gently brushed into an embossed cardstock surface with each color running into the next. The white stamped and embossed image on the white card resists the color and rises above the brushed color creating an intriguing texture.

MATERIALS

Rubber stamp: Magenta Onion Flowers
Cardstock: White
Printed paper: Magenta Turquoise Adornment,

Green Berry Branch
Cardboard tiles: Magenta
ColorBox ink: Frost White
Embossing powder:

White
Heat tool
Marvy Markers: Ochre, Plum, Pine Green
Brush and water

Stamp the image four times on white cardstock. Cover the images with white embossing powder, being sure to tap any excess powder back into the container. Set the embossing with a heat tool.

Brush water-based markers on a palette. Apply the ink by wetting the brush with lots of water, gathering some of the color from the palette, and brushing the color on the stamped, embossed cardstock. Apply the color quickly

because it dries fast. It might be best, if you are new to this technique, to complete one tile at a time, rather than trying to paint one color on each tile before moving to the next color.

While the faux watercolor is drying, prepare the four cardboard tiles. Cut the Turquoise Adornment printed paper to four 3-inch squares and cover the cardboard tiles with the cut paper, trimming the corners in a slight reverse arc to

prevent bulky folded corners from forming. Glue opposite sides first for a smooth fit of paper over the tile.

Cut each embossed tile just outside the border.

Mount the trimmed embossed tiles onto the wrapped cardboard tiles. Layer a 4½-inch square of Green Berry Branch printed paper on a 5¼-inch square card. Attach the four mounted cardboard tiles on the card.

Nathalie Métivier, Magenta

Layered Halloween Card

A zany ghost in red sneakers bars the door while his friends lean and fly out of windows in a wonderful Halloween haunted house. The palette is Halloween-perfect—an orange sky, purple ground, black die-cut house with yellow peeking through the windows and the fabulous smiling white ghosts with bright colored eyes and, of course, the one wearing the red sneakers.

MATERIALS

Card: Mrs. Grossman's Studio Cards Black haunted house

die cut Stickers: Mrs. Grossman's Tiny Ghosts

Cardstock: Orange, purple Adhesive

The black haunted house is the focal point with the silly little ghosts beckoning to us. "Boo!" says the card. Not scary, just delightful. The house is layered with foam mounting tape onto orange cardstock with a purple border at the bottom. The ghost stickers are cut as necessary to fit in the windows. A Halloween of fun.

Mrs. Grossman's Paper Company

72

Layered Gift Box

ittle Chubby Monsters cavort from an opened gift box—one foot in, one foot out—and seem to be screaming for joy. The layering is marvelous. Foam mounting tape lifts the package and the little monsters from the surface, adding dimension to the card.

MATERIALS

Cardstock: yellow, mauve, red, orange
Stickers: Mrs. Grossman's

Chubby Monsters, Sparkle Confetti, Pen & Ink Party Captions

Ribbon: Mrs. Grossman's Ribbon, Blue
Tweezers

The little monsters burst from the opened gift box with an explosion of confetti and teeth-baring smiles. The unusual colors set the tone for the madcap escapade—mauve, red, orange layer on a yellow card, complete with sparkling confetti.

Layer the mauve square on the yellow card. Tie a piece of the polka-dot blue ribbon around the box top and make a bow.

Attach the red box and the orange box top with foam mounting tape. Add three monsters as shown. The two at the top are just emerging from the box with feet partially in the box. Add the confetti using tweezers to place some in between the box and top.

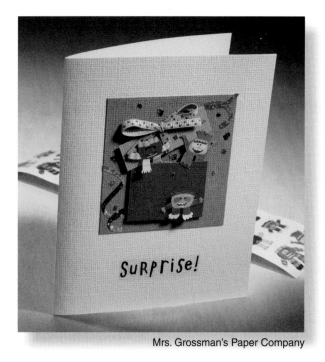

Mrs. Grossman's Paper Company

Layered and Popped Greetings

A simple centered composition is "popped" forward with foam mounting tape. A raspberry card supports a decorative-edged apricot panel which holds the featured lavender panel. The dimension and palette are fresh and appealing.

MATERIALS

Cardstock: Raspberry, apricot, lavender, yellow

Stickers: Card Captions, Encouragement; Scene One, Party Bear

Decorative-edge scissors
Foam mounting tape

Mrs. Grossman's Paper Company

A bear in a birthday party hat would be a welcome guest at any birthday celebration, specially a bear carrying a beautiful birthday cake.

Cut the edges of the apricot cardstock. Pop the bear and his cake on the lavender cardstock panel with foam mounting tape. Add the confetti stickers. Pop the message panel at the bottom of the lavender layer. And pop the decorated lavender panel on the apricot panel, and then onto the raspberry card.

Multi-layered Swiveling Card

One layer after another is cause for celebration. A fabulous card with an acetate layer of fireworks exploding over a layer of huge balloons layered over an array of small message tags rest on a large orange card base. Now this is a birthday card to remember!

MATERIALS

Stickers: Mrs. Grossman's Fireworks Silver & Gold; Sheer Color Heart Balloons; Card

Captions, Birthday
Cardstock: White, orange, purple, green, pink

Brad
Ruler
Craft knife
Cutting mat

The card is made in four layers. The bare orange cardstock, four ¾- by 5-inch panels with messages, a white panel with giant balloons, and on top an acetate layer with gold and silver exploding fireworks, all held together at the center top with an orange brad. The card layers can then swivel to either side.

Mrs. Grossman's Paper Company

75

Layered Move

A collage is a collection of artfully arranged images, papers, or other materials pasted together on a background. A collage can be assembled or constructed on the computer, as well as by hand. Scan and print found objects and layer the collage by hand, or scan and layer the collage on the computer. The results are amazing either way. A collection of fabric, ribbon, various papers, photographs, copper tag, and brad were scanned and assembled on the computer for this card. Windows were cut out of the fabric and family photographs placed in the windows. The button wheels were added to the printed card by hand. The envelope was made out of a scanned map.

Susan Swan

MATERIALS

Fabric	Photographs	Buttons
Printed paper	Brad	Thread
Painted paper	Copper tag	

Father's Day Collage

Old photos are a treasure. A father/grandfather photograph layered on a brick-red mat brings us right into the hearth with its warm palette and textured surfaces. The strong centered focal point of layered images captures our sense of family and keeping treasured family memories alive.

MATERIALS

Various papers
Fabrics
Newspaper

Photograph
Music
Sticker: Mr. Grossman's

red heart
Eyelets

A collage of an old photograph of father and grandfather, pieces of fabric with the bits of threads at the edges to create more detail and interest, music, old newspaper, painted paper is captivating. The ribbon is made of heavyweight paper printed with "Happy Father's Day" and is used to bind the collage together. The bright red heart at the bottom edge of the photograph states the message. The envelope is made from scans of two fabrics.

Susan Swan

Collaged Tags

These two collaged tags with different backgrounds look very different. The simple red mat presents the featured heart collage center-stage, while the stick frame takes the presentation to another level. We are as interested in the frame and background as we are in the collage.

MATERIALS

Handmade paper
Gold foil
Music score
Dried flowers

Metallic check paper
Sticks
Twine
Beads

Bristol board
Glue

Susan Swan

Layer metallic checkerboard paper on Bristol board or other heavy-weight stock, and trim to the appropriate shape. Create a frame with four small sticks bound together with twine.

Compose a small collage by cutting handmade paper into a heart shape, add a rectangle of gold foil, and layer ferns and a dried flower on top. Add a strip of music for the flower stem.

Mount the collage on the framed checkerboard paper for one version (left). Add a twine hanger with a dangling ornament with rolled hand-made paper and beads.

For the second version, mount the small collage onto a mat of red lightweight board. Add a red cord through a hole punched at the top of the tag.

Anniversary Collage

Here is a collage to simply admire. The artist has a small Mexican shadow box which she scanned and "tweaked" in Photoshop. Here are her words on the creation of this anniversary card in Photoshop: "I played with the levels and saturation to make the color a little more interesting, added details and the copper heart. I made a spine from a scan of the chalkboard used on the inside, and a dangle made up of handsome paper beads, milagros, and a glass bottle with part of a letter inside. The inside of the card is made from scanned photos, a sculpy heart—the color of which I changed in Photoshop; copper tag; and a scan of the window frame from the front of the shadow box was cut out, a sheet of acetate glued on and a cardboard frame added underneath to give it space enough so that it could be used as a pocket for letters and photos."

The collage was printed on heavy-weight paper and mounted onto light board. The shapes were cut with a craft knife and edges painted to match the paper colors.

Susan Swan

Computer-collaged card

An overall-muted palette with rich tonal highlights, textured pages, and torn edges offer a stunning collage created on the computer. An idea which we hope will inspire you to create your own collages of personal memories. This is all Susan Swan's artwork, many sections of which she created for other projects, saved on her computer to use again in this personal statement. Scanning and saving favorite papers and images is worth the effort.

Everything was assembled on the computer. Painted and gessoed papers, artwork, lace pieces, and type panels were scanned and then assembled with other scanned and saved pieces into this three-panel card.

What an extraordinary gift.

Susan Swan

4-leaf Collaged Card

Layers of flat, printed collaged backgrounds with dimensionally framed windows cut into each layer lead us to a focal point placed dramatically at the center of the last page of this four-leaf booklet-card. Three-dimensional texture layered on the printed texture; a refined, warm palette; and geometric shapes—squares, triangles, diamonds, and a central circle—are crucial to the dramatic effect. Love, the theme of the collage, is referenced on every page: in the warm palette, the text, and images.

Susan Swan

Each spread offers a collage of a different texture using the same palette. And each spread offers its own dimensionally framed window.

The movement and excitement of the collage is resolved in the simplicity of the final spread—a solid warm orange background presenting a simple orange and gray-green checkerboard mat supporting a small, framed circle with the text message.

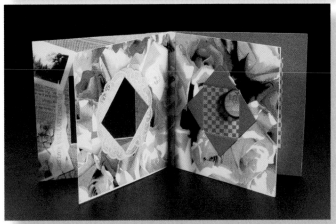

50th Anniversary Collage

Creating a collage gives an artist the opportunity to play with proportion, shape, color, and texture. This sumptuous collage of fabric and both printed and gouache-painted papers in a rich palette of swirling shapes (including the numeral "50" with subtle variations) and machine stitching is the basis for the accompanying card and small ornament/tag.

The artist created the collage, scanned it, and then used the scan to make the card and the stand-up ornament/tag on the computer. The finished card and the four faces of each ornament were then printed, the card on white cardstock, and the ornament images on photo paper.

The ornament is assembled from four reduced copies of the collage printed on sturdy, glossy photo paper. Two copies are mounted back-to-

back to make two two-sided panels. Cut a slit in each of the mounted pairs from the edge to the center point at the center line. Join the two pieces of one ornament to make a four-sided freestanding figure by sliding the center slit of one panel down the center slit of the second panel. The bottom edges of the panels will not align if you try to slide the uncut center of one panel down the cut panel of the other. Punch a hole at a top left corner. Add a ribbon to hang the ornament.

Christine Timmons

Christmas Collage 2007

An arrangement of fabric and gouache-on-paper snippets in a sophisticated palette presents rhythmic shapes, angled stitching, and an energetic composition. The artist used this collage as the basis for a card and small free-standing ornament. The ornament is created just like the ornament on the previous spread.

The textures are intriguing. Soft torn edges of some fabrics lie on soft painted paper, with machine stitching criss-crossing the layers. A narrow blue-green velvet ribbon cuts diagonally across the page, reiterating the stitching angles and some of the smaller shapes. The hard angles are balanced by several softer circle shapes.

Christine Timmons

QUILLING AND OTHE

R SPECIAL EFFECTS

We can bend, twist, fold, cut, tear, and otherwise
manipulate paper to create imaginative paper crafts,
and we can add additional decorative materials from
ribbons, needlework, small objects, and even more
manipulated papers, and other embellishments that
provide engaging special effects. Quilling, also known
as paper filigree, is all about texture and dimension
with its rolled long, narrow strips of paper. Ribbon
embroidery adds an elegant note to many paper craft
projects. And why not add a small gift—like earrings—
to a paper card? Embellishments need not be limited.

Quilled Oval Tags

Quilling is the art of rolling long, narrow strips of paper into coils that are arranged into decorative designs. Originating in Europe and spreading to England and then to the American colonies, quilling—or filigree—has been a favored pastime for centuries, adorning household objects such as tea caddies, trays, boxes, and even furniture. Our quilled designs add delicate notes of color and texture to many paper crafts.

MATERIALS

Quilling paper in various colors

Cardstock: White, green
Rubber stamp: Magenta

ColorBox Pigment inkpad: Hunter Green

Janet Williams

Cut white cardstock into four ovals, and stamp a stem image in hunter green ink on them. Quill ten half-circles in one color for each flower. Mount the ten half-circles, as face-to-face pairs, to form a circle above the stamped stem creating five petals for each flower. Quill four yellow loose coils and glue one to the center of each flower. Quill marquise shapes from longer paper for the leaves and attach them over the stamped stems.

Cut green cardstock with the larger oval template and trim the edges with decorative-edge scissors. Layer the

matted quilled ovals on the cut green cardstock.

For the note-card, place the smaller oval template at the lower left of the card. Trace the oval shape on the card and remove the template. Cut away approximately 1½ inches across the width of the card at the bottom edge, silhouetting the lower half of the traced oval shape. Ink the edges of the card. Attach one quilled, mounted panel onto the card, over the silhouetted shape.

Quilled Snowflake

A single subject, a quiet palette, and a simple arrangement combine to present a captivating project. There is nothing extraneous here: the three-dimensional snowflake centered on two layers of cardstock, one solid and one softly patterned, is without doubt the focal point.

MATERIALS

White quilling paper
Cardstock: Teal, light aqua, white

Patterned paper
Glass gems
Glue

Marvy Marker: Green
Corner punch
Gold leafing pen

Six decorative quilled designs are assembled to form the complete snowflake. Each design is composed of: one large off-center coil and three small glued coils for the "head," one closed heart, one marquise inside the heart, one small glued coil for each of the two arms and the body. The shapes are made with ⅛-inch strips of quilling paper, but longer strips are used for the body, creating larger shapes than those for the arms. The designs are arranged in a circle on mats of teal and light aqua cardstock, and patterned paper, and finally onto the white card.

Janet Williams

91

Basic Quilled Shapes

This swivel card offers an ingenious way to present a gift of a hand-made Christmas tree ornament. The right side of the card front is folded back on itself to the left edge to create a swivel. Create a quilled snowflake with ivory paper. The ornament is made with many tight coils. Color the top surface of the snowflake with a gold leafing pen and glue the snowflake to the polymer clay ornament. Following is a chart of some basic quilled shapes.

Roll the paper on the quilling tool to form a coil. Remove the coil from the tool. Allow the coil to relax and expand to desired size, and apply small amount of glue to the end of paper strip, gluing down to the coil.

Loose Glued Coil

Shaped Teardrop

Make a teardrop. Run your fingernail toward the point curling the point in one direction.

Roll the paper on the quilling tool to form a coil. DO NOT allow the coil to relax and expand. While the coil is still on the tool, apply small amount of glue to the end of paper strip, gluing down to the coil. Gently remove the coil from tool.

Tight Coil

Square

Make a loose glued coil. Pinch at one end of the coil to form a teardrop shape.

Make a loose glued coil. Flatten the coil between your fingers. Hold the flattened coil upright between thumb and index finger with the points at the top and bottom. Flatten again matching up the previous 2 folds created by the points. Reopen to form a square shape.

Half Circle

Make a loose glued coil. Flatten one side of the coil by pinching the circle at two points or flatten coil gently against your finger.

Teardrop

Triangle

Make a teardrop shape. Hold the teardrop at the pointed end between the thumb and index finger. Gently press the rounded end back until 3 points are formed.

Shaped Marquise

Make a marquise. Run your fingernail toward one point curling it up. Repeat at the other end curling in the opposite direction.

Marquise

Make a loose glued coil. Pinch at the exact opposite side of coil to form points at both ends, forming a marquise shape.

Open Heart

Fold a piece of paper in half. Rolling towards the center-fold, roll each end of paper inward toward the center-fold.

Rectangle

Make a loose glued coil. Flatten the coil between the fingers. Hold the flattened coil upright between thumb and index finger with points at the top and bottom. Slowly begin to flatten the coil once again moving the previous points slightly away from each other rather than matching them as in the square shape. Reopen to form a rectangle.

Bunny Ear

Make a loose glued coil. Gently push the coil against the quilling tool (1/4" diameter) to form a shape similar to the crescent, however with the 2 points closer together.

Holly Leaf

Make a loose glued coil. Flatten the coil between your fingers. Hold the flattened coil in the center tightly with tweezers. Gently push one end towards center with index finger and thumb forming 2 more points. Repeat on opposite end. Reshape as needed.

Rolled Heart (Arrow)

Make a teardrop. Hold the teardrop shape between the thumb and index finger of one hand. Gently push the center of rounded end back using the straight edge of the tweezers. Crease at both sides of the pushed-in end.

Crescent

Make a teardrop. Pinch one more point not quite opposite of the first point. Run your fingernail toward both points curling the points up or make a loose glued coil. Press coil against the rounded side of the quilling tool or finger to give the coil a crescent shape.

"V" Shape

Fold the paper in half. Curl each end of paper away from center-fold forming semi-tight coils at each end.

Quilling Shapes and Instructions by Janet Williams

Quilled Butterfly Tags

Gift wrapping can be almost as exciting as the gift inside. With gift tags like these, perhaps you don't really need much more of a gift: These are enough. At any rate, the tags make a real statement.

MATERIALS

White cardstock
⅛-inch quilling paper
Rubber stamp: Magenta

Moss green inkpad
Quilling tool
Olive green eyelet

Eyelet tool
Glue
Gold leafing pen

Janet Williams

Charming quilled butterflies "Just fluttering by to say, Hi!" adorn two gift tags. A moss-green stamped image creates the ground for the yellow, gold-leafed butterflies on each tag. The body and wings for the butterflies are all marquise shapes. The antenna is a V-shape. Cut the white cardstock into two tag shapes. Stamp them. Glue the quilled butterflies to the stamped tags. Add the eyelets and gold cord.

Quilled Dragonfly Card

Delicate scrollwork on a soft gray-yellow-green palette presents a refreshing minimalist example of quilling. A portion of a daisy on a barely yellow square and a dragonfly hovering over a pale summer-green ground brings us right into summer. Provo Craft Qwikit provides the kit containing the card, mats, and inks.

The quilled dragonfly is made with four white marquise shapes for the wings, a very long green marquise for the body, and two tiny green, tight, glued coils for the antennae.

The green-stamped background includes a trio of dragonflies in flight. The central figure is embellished with the quilled dragonfly glued right on top of the stamped figure.

The half daisy is glued on the small yellow square. Layer the small matted quilled panel at the lower right section of the card.

Janet Williams

95

Quilled Rose Window

A profusion of sumptuous quilled mauve and cream roses arranged on a nest of green leaves is seen through a double-matted window in the front of this triple panel card. A thin gold rule about ¼ inch around the window defines the top layer of the card.

MATERIALS

Cardstock: Cream (15 by 6½-inch, folded twice to form a 5-by 6½-inch-card with two inside pages), mauve, and green
Quilling paper: Mauve, cream, and two shades of green
Quilling tool
Leaf punch
Marker: dark green
Gold pen
Glue

Hold the quilling tool perpendicular in the right hand. Thread the quilling paper onto tool from the left side, with the paper horizontal to the tool. Roll the paper towards the left until you have made 1½ complete turns around the tool.

Making your first fold: With the left hand, fold the paper down towards your body. The quilling paper should now be perpendicular against the tool, both going in the same direction. Hold the paper firmly in the left hand and rotate your right arm up while holding the tool. This should make the paper form a

"cone" shape on the end of the tool. Bring your right arm back down making sure to

keep the "cone" shape. For the rest of the folds: Repeat the same instructions used for the first fold until you are at the end of your strip of paper. Generally 3 inches of

paper will yield 7-9 folds.

Final forming of rose: Remove your folded rose from the tool. Using a pair of pointed tweezers, hold the very center of the rose & gently turn the paper outward, the oppo-

site way you originally folded the paper. This opens up the rose slightly. Gently fold the

petals of the rose down by grabbing several layers of

folds with the tweezers and pulling them down away from the center of the rose. The "crushed" look actually does

come from gently "smashing" the rose between two fingers before gluing it into place.

Instructions courtesy Janet Williams.

The quilled lavish bouquet design is attached to the first inside page and spills out of the double-matted window cut in the front of the card. The window is actually cut in the center panel to reveal the quilled artwork mounted on the second panel.

Janet Williams

Ribbon Embroidery

Soft violet ribbon-embroidered roses and greenery are decidedly feminine and romantic embellishments for a card. The pattern for each rose is created by piercing and stitching with embroidery thread a five-point star-shape grid. The ribbon is anchored at the center of the pattern and wound alternately over and under each spoke around the circle.

MATERIALS

Cardstock: lilac, white
Punch: decorative corner trim
Ribbon: violet
Embroidery thread: green

Glue
Hole punch or awl
Tweezers

Irene Seifer

Cut and fold lilac cardstock into a 5-inch square top-folded card. Cut a second piece of lilac cardstock to a 3-inch square. Cut white cardstock to a 4½-inch square panel, and a 2½-inch square panel.

Punch two holes in one corner of the smaller white cardstock panel. Create the embroidery grid (a star shape with an uneven number of points and a center dot). Mark the grid in pencil on the white cardstock panel. Stitch from each point of the star into the center using embroidery thread. Anchor the ribbon at the center of the grid and wind it over and under each thread spoke around the circle. The uneven number of points insures alternate over- and under-steps.

Stems and leaves are green embroidery thread. Slip a lilac ribbon in and out of the two punched holes at the top of the cardstock panel, and tie a bow.

Layer the panels.

Ornament Card

Knowing the purpose of a project is the first step in the design process. For whom and why are you creating the card? What do you want the recipient to feel when he or she receives it? The purpose will help you choose appropriate materials, a meaningful palette, and an appealing composition.

MATERIALS

Sculpy polymer clay
Red acrylic paint
Vellum

Gray cardstock
Ribbon
Computer

A polymer clay ornament embellishes a simple, understated card created to celebrate the first wedding anniversary of a family member. The elegant palette of gray and red and the simple centered composition on the square card contribute to a pleasing presentation.

The sculpy heart is tied onto the gray card with ribbon. The two vellum bands were printed and used to wrap around the card and the envelope. The sculpy heart on the envelope vellum wrap was scanned and printed on sticker paper. The heart sticker holds the vellum strip together. Less is more.

Susan Swan

99

Dimensional Butterfly

A teal blue butterfly with wings lifted off the surface of the card brings added texture and depth to the card. Embellishments lift a composition, giving it added dimension, a little extra spice.

MATERIALS

Magenta rubber stamps: Butterflies, Butterfly
White cardstock
Magenta printed paper:

Blueberry Branch
ColorBox pigment ink: Frost White, Teal
ColorBox pigment ink

Mist Petal Point
White embossing powder
Heat tool

Susan Swan

1. Stamp the butterflies pattern on four 2-inch square white cardstock panels with white pigment ink. Emboss two stamped squares with white embossing powder. Color with Celadon and Robin's Egg petals from the Mist Petal Point package. Rub off the excess ink with a dry paper towel. Color the remaining two stamped squares with Aqua and Peacock pigment ink, and rub off any excess with a dry paper towel.

Stamp the butterfly with white pigment ink on to a piece of white cardstock, and emboss with white embossing powder.

2. Mount the four inked squares on a white cardstock square.

3. Layer the blueberry branch printed paper on a square white card, and layer the matted four-tile panels on top of the printed paper.

4. Silhouette the single stamped and embossed butterfly. Attach to the center of the card, and lift the wings slightly off the surface for an interesting dimension.

Flower Embellishments

The texture of a simple decorative ornamentation can add an unexpected lift to a project. A broken surface has more visual weight than a smooth one. This card offers simple shapes, palette, and composition with the added texture offering diversity.

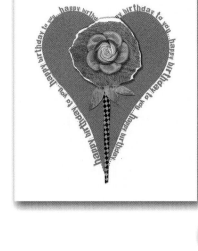

Susan Swan

From the LEFT: "For You" is a collage of a flower made out of cut and torn painted papers, checkerboard wrapping paper, and text printed from the computer. The card has a glossy black cover, sprayed with a little varnish to prevent smudges. The words "for you" were printed on the same paper as that used inside and glued above and below the window to offer contrast with the papers. MIDDLE: The heart shape offers a vintage button layered onto torn painted papers and a metallic check printed paper. The text in the shape of a heart was composed and printed on the computer. RIGHT: The Happy Birthday Tag offers a Happy Birthday message printed on the computer, a fabric flower with a mini button, and a strip of polka-dot fabric for a stem. An eyelet holds the hanging cord.

Earring Mom

Crafting is about communicating and having fun. How lucky that the recipient of this card has someone who appreciates her fun-loving nature. And the card is a card and gift at the same time: the earrings that dangle from Mom's paper ears are real. The lace, button eyes, and small fabric rose are also real. The rest of the card was created on the computer, printed, and constructed.

The image at left below shows all the elements of the card: a strip of checkerboard paper, a strip of lace, a small silk rose, painted letters "M o m," a piece of a scanned flower painting, and the painted paper card with the special fold on the front. Next is the head with earrings in place, followed by the finished head with cut-paper hair and button eyes. And finally the assembled card. You *do* have to smile. Crafting is about celebrating life and having fun, and we should have fun making cards for friends and family. Certainly they have fun receiving them.

Susan Swan

Wedding Invitations

S oft, romantic colors, gentle shapes, and imaginative paper cutting all add up to a wedding invitation. The shapes and colors are assimilated into each element of the invitation package

MATERIALS

Cardstock: ivory
Vellum; white
Paper: printer, ivory

Envelopes: moss green
Ribbon: lilac
Twine: violet

Decorative edge scissors
Eyelets: rose

Susan Swan

Susan Swan

These elegant invitations were created on the computer. The fabulous paper was created by the artist and scanned for the background for the invitation. The edges are distressed. The file is printed and trimmed to a square. A sheet of vellum protects the printed square in the envelope. The gatefold card enclosing the invitation is held closed with soft cord wrapped around lovely paper buttons cut from the decorative paper used on the card inside, decorated with the initials of the bride and groom, and attached to each panel of the envelope with eyelets for added dimension. The same button shape cut with decorative-edge scissors bearing the words "I Do" closes the outer envelope. The two versions are similar in feeling—soft, romantic, and contemporary. They share the double-horizontal-fold format, torn edges, and paper buttons. The orange-and-blue bouquet version incorporates ribbon and a tiny framed photo of the couple. The soft pink version offers a full painted background image while the orange and blue has a silhouetted bouquet.

Templates

DIAMOND FOLD, P. 45

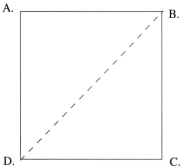

1. Fold the square in half diagonally.
   Crease and unfold.

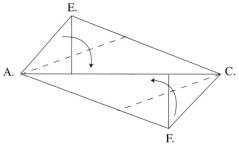

3. Fold the A-E side to center.
   Fold the C-F side to center.

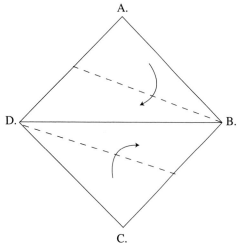

1. Rotate square 45° so point A is at
   top. Fold the A-B side in to center.
   Fold the C-D side to center.

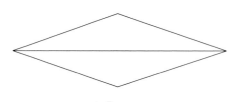

4. Turn over.

STAR SQUARE FOLD, P. 46

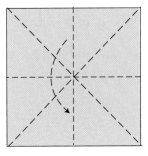

1. Start with a square of paper and fold in half horizontally. Crease and unfold. Fold in half vertically. Crease and unfold. Fold in half diagonally both ways, creasing and unfolding each time.

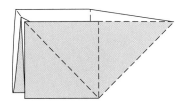

3. Squash the left triangle tip behind the front square. Squash the right triangle tip behind the square.

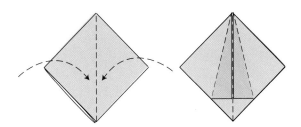

5. Fold the top layer on each side in the center.

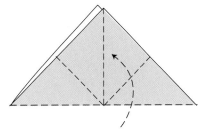

2. Turn paper with point up.

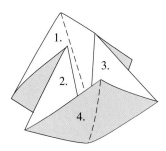

4. Flatten the square with point up and two layers on each side.

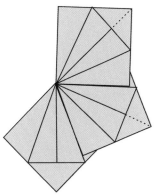

6. Interlock: Slip the left point of the bottom layer of one piece under the top layer of another; repeat with all eightfolded diamonds. Dot glue in folds to secure.

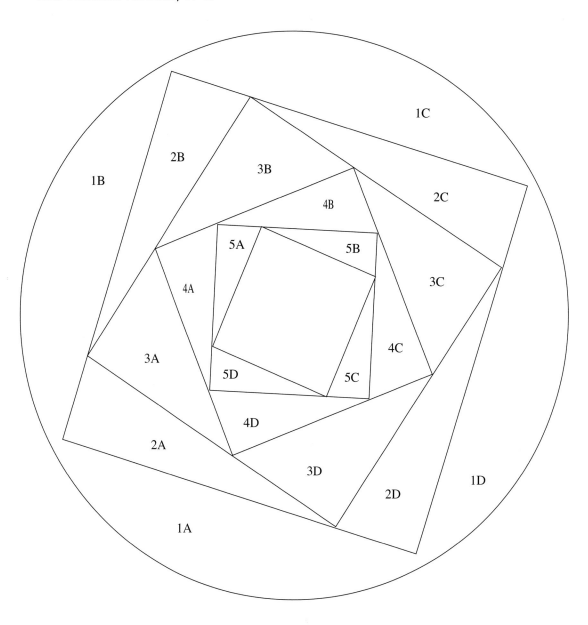

IRIS FOLDING PATTERN, P. 47

1C
2B
3B
1B
4B
2C
5A
5B
4A
3C
5D
5C
3A
4C
2A
4D
3A
3D
1A
2D
1D

SELF-FOLDING ENVELOPE, P. 33

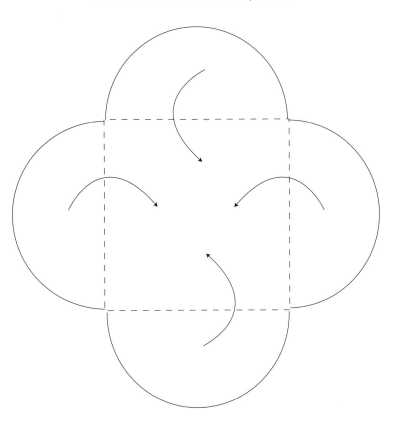

FOLIO POCKET, P. 23

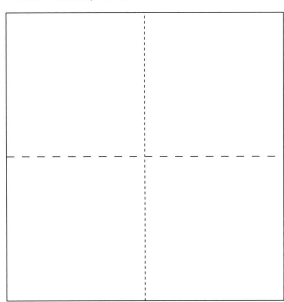

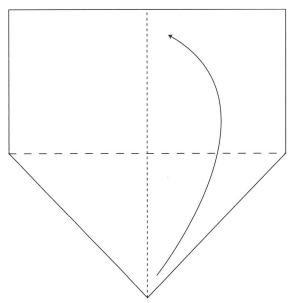

POP-UP TEMPLATE, P. 38

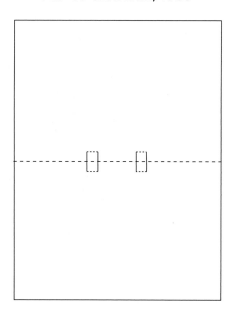

CHRISTMAS TREE WINDOW, P. 40

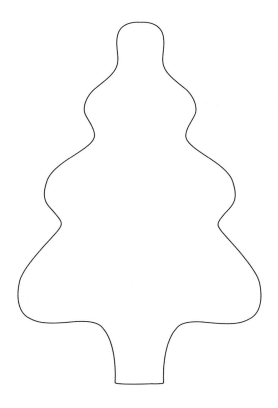

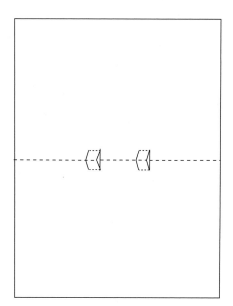

Illustrated Glossary of Techniques

 **ACCORDION FOLDING** Accordion folding is the technique of creating a succession of alternating mountain and valley folds across a sheet of paper. You can make cards or small booklets with accordion folds. See page 28.

 **EMBOSSING, INK** Ink-embossing is the process of making an inked image three-dimensional by applying a special powder which, when heated, rises up and becomes permanent. See page 70.

 **GATE-FOLD** A gate-folded card has the opening fold at the center of the card so that you turn back both sides to reveal the interior. See page 104.

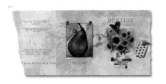 **COLLAGE** Collage is a collection of artfully arranged images, papers, or other materials, pasted together on a page, card or other project. See page 80.

 **FAUX ENAMEL FINISH** A faux enamel finish can be created by adding small dollops of glistening clear lacquer to embossed images. See page 18.

 **HAND-PAINTED PAPERS** Hand-painted papers created with any kind of paint add depth and interest to the card. See page 40.

 **CUT-PAPER ARTWORK** Cut-paper is a technique of cutting and layering paper to create images with color, texture, and depth. See page 52.

 **FOLDED-PAPER CUTTING** Folded-paper cutting lets you create a perfect symmetrical design. Fold a piece of paper in half, sketch one half of a design at the folded edge and cut it out. When you unfold the paper, you have a complete, symmetrical design. See page 57.

 **IRIS FOLDING** Iris folding involves arranging folded strips of paper in a spiral pattern around a central opening, similar to the iris of the eye or the lens of a camera. See page 47.

PAPER FOLDING   With just a few carefully placed folds you can create imaginative three-dimensional shapes of varying levels of complexity. See page 32.

PUNCH ART   Punch art is the process of using punched shapes flat, or combining them to create new images. Both the positive (punched shape) and the negative shape can be useful. See page 65.

TEA-BAG FOLDING   Tea-bag folding, similar to origami, is the art of folding small squares of paper into interesting shapes that are artfully arranged in a pleasing pattern. See page 45.

PAPER LAYERING   Paper layering is placing light paper, like vellum or acetate, over an image to soften it; or arranging multiple decorated papers one on top of another. See page 75.

QUILLING   Quilling is an elegant decorative technique accomplished by rolling thin strips of paper around a needle tool into various shapes and then combining these shapes to embellish artwork. See page 94.

TORN PAPER   Paper is itself an extraordinarily versatile embellishment. The soft, uneven edge of torn paper adds grace, color, and depth to a project. See page 62.

POP-UP CONSTRUCTION   Pop-up construction is the art of cutting, folding, and mounting an image so that when you open a card the design literally pops up from the inside. See page 43.

RIBBON EMBROIDERY   Ribbon embroidery is the art of creating dimensional details by stitching with narrow ribbon to add color, texture, and depth. See page 98.

WINDOW CARDS   Window cards are created by cutting appropriate-size openings in one or more panels of a folded card, to reveal artwork visible through the cut opening. See page 34.

DATE DUE	